IPO 2010E001

February 1, 2010

Inspector General

United States
Department *of* Defense

Evaluation of DoD Sexual Assault Response in
Operations Enduring and Iraqi Freedom Areas of
Operation

Additional Information and Copies

The Department of Defense Office of the Deputy Inspector General for Policy and Oversight, Assistant Inspector General for Investigative Policy and Oversight, prepared this report. If you have questions or would like to obtain additional copies, contact Ms. Melvina Coakley at (703) 604-8622 (DSN 664-8622).

Suggestions for Evaluations

To suggest ideas for or to request future evaluations, contact the Office of the Deputy Inspector General for Auditing at (703) 604-9142 (DSN 664-9142) or fax (703) 604-8932. Ideas and requests can also be mailed to:

> ODIG-AUD (ATTN: Audit Suggestions)
> Department of Defense Inspector General
> 400 Army Navy Drive (Room 801)
> Arlington, VA 22202-4704

DEPARTMENT OF DEFENSE

To report fraud, waste, mismanagement, and abuse of authority.

Send written complaints to: Defense Hotline, The Pentagon, Washington, DC 20301-1900
Phone: 800.424.9098   e-mail: hotline@dodig.mil   www.dodig.mil/hotline

Acronyms and Abbreviations

Acronym	Refers to:	Acronym	Refers to:
AFOSI	Air Force Office of Special Investigations	MNC-I	Multi National Corps-Iraq
DoD	Department of Defense	MNF-I	Multi National Force-Iraq
FAR	Federal Acquisition Regulation	NCIS	Naval Criminal Investigative Service
HCP	Health Care Provider	OUSD (P&R)	Office of the Under Secretary of Defense (Personnel and Readiness)
IG	Inspector General	SAFE	Sexual Assault Forensic Examination
KBR	Kellogg Brown & Root	SAPRO	Sexual Assault Prevention and Response Office
MCCID	Marine Corps Criminal Investigation Division	SARC	Sexual Assault Response Coordinator
MCIO	Military Criminal Investigative Organization	USCENTCOM	United States Central Command
MEJA	Military Extraterritorial Jurisdiction Act of 2000	VA	Victims Advocate

INSPECTOR GENERAL
DEPARTMENT OF DEFENSE
400 ARMY NAVY DRIVE
ARLINGTON, VIRGINIA 22202-4704

FEB - 1 2010

MEMORANDUM FOR UNDER SECRETARY OF DEFENSE (PERSONNEL AND READINESS)

SUBJECT: Evaluation of DoD Sexual Assault Response In Operations Enduring and Iraqi Freedom Areas of Operation (Report No. IPO2010E001)

This final report is provided for your review and comment. Management comments on the previous draft report were considered in completing this report, and are included in their entirety as Appendix F.

Your office concurred with our recommendations and advised that implementation actions have already begun. In commenting on this final report, we ask that you include estimated completion dates for the actions. Please submit your comments electronically within 30 days to melvina.coakley@dodig.mil.

We appreciate the courtesies extended to the review staff. For additional information on this report, please contact Ms. Melvina Coakley, (703) 604-8622; 664-8622 (DSN). You may also contact Mr. John Perryman, Director of Oversight, at (703) 604-8765; 664-8765 (DSN).

FOR: Charles W. Beardall
Deputy Inspector General
for Policy and Oversight

Attachment
Final Report IPO2010E001

IPO2010E001

TABLE OF CONTENTS

EVALUATION OF DOD SEXUAL ASSAULT RESPONSE IN OPERATIONS ENDURING AND IRAQI FREEDOM AREAS OF OPERATION

I. INTRODUCTION AND SUMMARY

We initiated this review in response to questions from Members of Congress concerning Department of Defense (DoD) sexual assault[1] policies for contractor personnel[2] in combat areas. Our review sought to determine whether DoD policies and practices ensure sexual assault complaints involving contractors in the Operations Enduring Freedom and Iraqi Freedom areas of operation were properly received, processed, and referred for investigation.[3] We focused on the following specific questions:

A. Do DoD policies and procedures address receiving, processing, and reporting sexual assault complaints involving contractor personnel in the areas of operation?

B. Are military medical officials required to report sexual assault complaints from contractor personnel to law enforcement personnel?

---

[1] DoD Directive 6495.01, "Sexual Assault Prevention and Response (SAPR) Program," October 6, 2005, states that "for the purpose of this Directive and SAPR awareness training and education, the term "sexual assault" is defined as intentional sexual contact, characterized by use of force, physical threat or abuse of authority or when the victim does not or can not consent. It includes rape, nonconsensual sodomy (oral or anal sex), indecent assault (unwanted, inappropriate sexual contact or fondling), or attempts to commit these acts. Sexual assault can occur without regard to gender or spousal relationship or age of victim. "Consent" shall not be deemed or construed to mean the failure by the victim to offer physical resistance. Consent is not given when a person uses force, threat of force, coercion, or when the victim is asleep, incapacitated, or unconscious." Change 1, November 2008, has updated this definition and states "that the term "sexual assault" is defined as intentional sexual contact, characterized by use of force, threats, intimidation, abuse of authority, or when the victim does not or cannot consent. Sexual assault includes rape, forcible sodomy (oral or anal sex), and other unwanted sexual contact that is aggravated, abusive, or wrongful (to include unwanted and inappropriate sexual contact), or attempts to commit these acts. "Consent" means words or overt acts indicating a freely given agreement to the sexual conduct at issue by a competent person. An expression of lack of consent through words or conduct means there is no consent. Lack of verbal or physical resistance or submission resulting from the accused's use of force, threat of force, or placing another person in fear does not constitute consent. A current or previous dating relationship by itself or the manner of dress of the person involved with the accused in the sexual conduct at issue shall not constitute consent."

[2] For purposes of this review, the terms "contractor," "contractor personnel," "civilian," and "civilian personnel" are defined as persons employed by the DoD or Defense contractors who are U.S. citizens.

[3] The Office of the Inspector General of the Department of Defense also conducted an "Audit of DoD and DoD Contractor Efforts to Prevent Sexual Assault/Harassment Involving Contractor Employees Within Operations Enduring Freedom and Iraqi Freedom Areas of Operation" (Project No. D2008-DOOOCE-0221.000).

C. Do military medical officials comply with standards regarding forensic examinations and medical records maintenance?

D. What are the dispositions of complainants and accused personnel during the investigative process when sexual assault complaints involve contractor personnel?

The DoD Sexual Assault Prevention and Response program policy for sexual assault response, as outlined in DoD Directive 6495.01, "Sexual Assault Prevention and Response (SAPR) Program," October 6, 2005, is to (1) provide an immediate, trained response capability for each sexual assault report in all locations, including deployed locations, and (2) ensure sexual assault victims are protected, treated with dignity and respect, and receive timely access to appropriate treatment and services. This policy is implemented at the Military Service level in Service specific regulations, and through the use of Sexual Assault Response Coordinators (SARC), Deployed Sexual Assault Response Coordinators (DSARC), Victim Advocates (VA), Health Care Providers (HCP), and law enforcement personnel.

To evaluate the DoD response to contractor sexual assault complaints, we reviewed current and past policies and procedures for reporting a sexual assault involving a contractor. We interviewed representatives from the offices responsible for, and people in the field who implement, the DoD Sexual Assault Prevention and Response Program. We also interviewed officials with the Office of the Under Secretary of Defense (Personnel and Readiness), Sexual Assault Prevention and Response Office (SAPRO), the office that administers the sexual assault program, and officials from the Military Service Sexual Assault Prevention and Response programs, the offices that implement the program.

Our interviews included key personnel, such as the SARC. These individuals serve as the central points of contact to oversee sexual assault awareness, prevention, and response training and to ensure appropriate care is coordinated and provided to sexual assault complainants. We also interviewed DSARCs who function as SARCs in combat environments; VAs who facilitate care for complainants under the Sexual Assault Prevention and Response program; and HCPs who provide health care services at Military Medical Treatment Facilities. They, along with law enforcement officers, are collectively known as first responders. We considered these entities to be an integral part of the DoD program for receiving, processing, and reporting sexual assaults.

We found one major policy deficiency during our review. The DoD policies and processes for receiving, processing, and reporting sexual assaults address only active duty Service members and other individuals authorized treatment in a Military Medical Treatment Facility.[4] The policies do not address other categories of personnel, such as DoD civilian and contractor personnel who deploy with military forces.

---

[4] Eligibility for treatment is determined by the Military Services and reported to the Defense Enrollment Eligibility Reporting System. Eligibility is usually limited to Service members, retirees, and their family members.

To remedy this lack of program guidance, deployed commanders implemented local procedures to care for all sexual assault complainants. Those procedures took the complainant's status into account in determining whether program differences, e.g., restricted[5] and unrestricted[6] reporting requirements, should be applied in individual cases.

After reviewing investigative files and other records, and interviewing or surveying 133 SARCs, DSARCs, VAs, and commanders, we learned the Military Services, though lacking definitive SAPRO guidance, routinely provided victim services to sexual assault complainants, including U.S. civilian and contractor personnel. These services included emergency care, follow-on care, and referring the complaint for investigation. Consequently, sexual assault complainants involved in the U.S. deployments received investigative, medical, and advocacy services when the sexual assault was reported to military officials. We did not find any evidence or instance where the Military Services denied Sexual Assault Prevention and Response program services to contractor personnel.

We did find that the SAPRO, Military Service Sexual Assault Prevention and Response program officials, and local DSARCs did not collect, document, or report advocacy services information provided to civilian and contractor employees. Therefore, we could not analyze primary records on advocacy services these complainants may have received. During calendar years 2005 through 2007, the Military Criminal Investigative Organizations (MCIOs)[7] conducted 25 sexual assault investigations involving U.S. civilian and contractor personnel in the Operations Enduring and Iraqi Freedom areas of operation.

In 8 of the 25 cases (32 percent), contractor company officials reported the assault to DoD military authorities. In the remaining 17 cases (68 percent), the complainants notified law enforcement directly, either through a friend, a co-worker, or the military chain of command. In nine cases (36 percent), medical personnel performed sexual assault forensic examinations, and provided evidence to criminal investigators.

In 12 cases (48 percent), the criminal investigative files indicated the victims were offered either SARC or Employee Assistance Program services.[8] In addition, these files included notes or coordination records, indicating SARC or Employee Assistance

---

[5] Per DoD Directive 6495.01, restricted reporting allows a Service member to disclose, confidentially, the details of his/her sexual assault to specified individuals and receive medical treatment, counseling, and advocacy services without triggering the official investigative process. This option is only available to Service members.

[6] Per DoD Directive 6495.01, unrestricted reporting allows an individual to report the details of his/her sexual assault and receive medical treatment, counseling, and advocacy services, but the report triggers the official investigative process.

[7] The MCIOs include the U.S. Army Criminal Investigation Command, the Naval Criminal Investigative Service, and the Air Force Office of Special Investigations.

[8] Professional support services provided to employees by the Defense contractor usually through a private insurer.

Program representatives were present during complainant interviews with law enforcement.

We found no DoD or Service-specific policy that required military medical officials to report sexual assault complaints to law enforcement authorities. DoD policy[9] describes the medical provider's role as notifying the SARC. The policy stipulates that the medical provider's notification requirement is met once the SARC has been notified, and the SARC will handle reporting to law enforcement.

We found medical officials complied with DoD standards for collecting, preserving, and maintaining chain of custody over evidence, specifically using Sexual Assault Forensic Examination kits. Additionally, the Military Services regulatory requirements for collecting Sexual Assault Forensic Examination kits complied with DoD policy. In the 25 cases reviewed, we did not identify any instance where a sexual assault forensic examination was appropriate, but not conducted.

Finally, we found that available data provided a final disposition on the accused once the allegation was adjudicated. However, records did not indicate the disposition of the complainant or the accused during the investigative process.

We recommend the Under Secretary of Defense (Personnel and Readiness), establish, and the Military Services implement, policy that will provide an immediate response, by trained personnel, for all sexual assaults involving U.S. personnel reported to DoD facilities.

We also recommend the Under Secretary of Defense (Personnel and Readiness), Sexual Assault Prevention and Response Program Office, in coordination with the Military Services develop a data system that records relevant data on sexual assault cases involving civilian and contractor personnel. The data, at minimum, should include the complainant's identity, when and where the assault occurred, when the complaint was filed, the support services requested or provided, when the complaint was referred for criminal investigation, and the final disposition on the complaint.

This report sets forth our detailed findings and recommendations based on reviewing the existing DoD policy, guidance, and practice.

II.   BACKGROUND

In a letter to, and in testimony before the Congress, Ms. Jaime Leigh Jones stated that on July 28, 2005, while working in Iraq for Kellogg Brown and Root (KBR), other KBR employees sexually assaulted her.[10] At the time, Ms. Jones worked at Camp Hope, Iraq, an area under the operational control of the United States Department of State. The

---

[9]   DoD Pamphlet, "Healthcare Provider's Role in Responding to Sexual Assault."

[10]   Jamie Leigh Jones' May 16, 2007, letter to Senator Charles Grassley, and December 19, 2007, "Testimony before the House Judiciary Subcommittee on Crime, Terrorism and Homeland Security."

Department of State Bureau of Diplomatic Security investigated her sexual assault complaint[11] and presented the case to the U.S. Attorney for the Northern District of Florida, who accepted the case on June 1, 2007. We limited our work on Ms. Jones' complaint to the DoD response to her sexual assault complaint.[12] The results of our work are at Appendix A.

As a result of Ms. Jones's contacts, we received numerous congressional requests to evaluate how DoD responds when Government contractor personnel working in Iraq and Afghanistan complain they have been sexually assaulted.

III. SCOPE

To evaluate the DoD response to sexual assault complaints in Iraq and Afghanistan, we reviewed the legislative requirements relative to the DoD sexual assault policy, as well as past and current DoD and Military Services policies, regulations, and procedures. We also examined reports that included previous findings and recommendations related to sexual assault in the Military Services and at Service Academies. For the current review, we focused on how DoD responds to sexual assault complaints involving contract employees who accompany U.S. Forces in Iraq and Afghanistan.

We interviewed Office of the Secretary of Defense, United States Central Command (USCENTCOM), and Military Services officials responsible for the Sexual Assault Prevention and Response program, including: DoD SAPRO staff; Departments of the Army, Navy, Air Force, and Marine Corps Sexual Assault Prevention and Response Program Directors and staffs; USCENTCOM Sexual Assault Prevention and Response Program Director and staff; and Major Command, Numbered Command, Fleet Command, and installation and deployed SARCs. We also conducted focus group meetings, and interviewed and surveyed current and former DSARCs, Installation Victim Advocates, Unit Victim Advocates, HCPs, and other medical personnel.

Additionally, to evaluate DoD visibility over sexual assault incidents involving contractors, we reviewed all criminal investigative files the MCIOs identified as involving contractor personnel who filed a sexual assault complaint between January 2005 and December 2007. (See Appendix C for case information).

---

[11] We did not review Ms. Jones' complaint as part of the 25 sexual assault investigations involving DoD civilian and contractor personnel because DoD criminal investigators did not conduct the investigation.

[12] At the request of the U.S. Attorney's office, we did not initiate our work on the DoD response until after the U.S. Attorney's office completed their work. The Department of Justice notified us on April 10, 2009, its work was completed.

IV.   FINDINGS AND ANALYSIS

A. Do DoD policies and procedures address receiving, processing, and reporting sexual assault complaints for contractor personnel in Iraq and Afghanistan?

We concluded DoD does not have official policies or procedures for sexual assault advocacy services and attendant medical services for contractors in Iraq and Afghanistan. Legislation required that DoD establish a comprehensive sexual assault policy for Service members. The DoD program is only for Service members and individuals eligible for treatment in a military medical treatment facility. As a matter of practice, however, the Military Services have provided Sexual Assault Prevention and Response Program services to contractor sexual assault complainants in Iraq and Afghanistan. We did not find any evidence or instance where the Military Services denied sexual assault response services to contractors.

1.   Standards

The applicable standards are from 10 U.S.C. §113 note (2008), "Department of Defense Policy and Procedures on Prevention and Response to Sexual Assaults Involving Members of Armed Forces;" DoD Directive (DoDD) 6495.01, "Sexual Assault Prevention and Response Program," October 6, 2005; DoD Instruction (DoDI) 6495.02, "Sexual Assault Prevention and Response Program," June 23, 2006; Army Regulation (AR) 600-208, "Army Command Policy," March 20, 2008; "Department of the Air Force Instruction 36-6001; Sexual Assault Prevention and Response (SAPR) Program," September 29, 2008; Operational Navy Instruction (OPNAVINST) 1752.1B,"The Sexual Assault Victim Intervention (SAVI) Program," December 29, 2006; and Marine Corps Order (MCO) 1752.5, "Sexual Assault Prevention and Response Program," February 05, 2008. These standards are detailed in Appendix B.

2.   Facts

DoD Policies and Procedures. In examining the DoD Sexual Assault Prevention and Response Program, we interviewed SAPRO officials, Military Service Sexual Assault Prevention and Response Program officials, deployed commanders and their staffs, and current and former deployed SARCs, DSARCs, and VAs from Iraq and Afghanistan. Our specific focus was to determine how DoD personnel responded to, processed, and referred for investigation, sexual assault complaints involving U.S. contractor employees.

In October 2004, Congress passed legislation[13] requiring DoD to develop a comprehensive policy on the prevention and response to sexual assaults involving

---

[13] "Ronald W. Reagan National Defense Authorization Act for Fiscal Year 2005, 108 Pub. L. 375, 118 Stat. 1811, div. A, title V. §577 Department of Defense Policy and Procedures on Prevention and Response to Sexual Assaults Involving Members of the Armed Forces, Oct. 28, 2004, 118 Stat. 1926 (10 U.S.C. §113 note), as amended by National Defense Authorization Act for Fiscal Year 2006, 109

Service members. The policy was to provide a foundation for DoD to improve sexual assault prevention, enhance support to victims, and increase reporting and accountability for active duty Service members. The legislation also required a restricted reporting option for Service members.

In addition, the law required that the Military Services develop or modify regulations to include a program promoting sexual assault awareness; provide victim advocacy and intervention services for Service members, at home and in deployed locations; and establish procedures for Service members to follow after a sexual assault incident. DoD promulgated its Sexual Assault Prevention and Response program guidance and established the SAPRO to address sexual assault policy.

The SAPRO, under direction from the Under Secretary of Defense (Personnel and Readiness), is the DoD proponent for sexual assault policy and oversight. The SAPRO serves as the single point for responsibility and oversight in sexual assault policy, providing guidance to DoD components and resolving issues common to the Military Services and joint commands.

The legislation required, and DoD guidance established, sexual assault prevention and response capabilities specifically for Service members. As such, SAPRO focused its sexual assault policies on active duty Service members only. In October 2005, DoD published a directive, and in June 2006, published an implementing instruction establishing DoD policy and procedures for sexual assault response for Service members.[14] Also in June 2006, DoD published new instructions establishing two sexual assault reporting options for Service members – those for restricted and unrestricted reporting.[15] DoD procedures required the Military Services to establish an around-the-clock sexual assault response capability for Service members, regardless of their location, that would ensure optimal and safe administration of unrestricted and restricted reporting options, with appropriate protection, medical care, counseling and advocacy.

The Sexual Assault Prevention and Response Program provides an unrestricted and restricted reporting option. An unrestricted report occurs when a Service member complains about a sexual assault and desires medical treatment, counseling, and an official investigation. A restricted report occurs when a Service member complains about a sexual assault but does not wish to trigger an official investigation. When notified about either type report, the SARC immediately assigns a victim advocate. Additionally,

---

Pub. L. 163, 119 Stat. 3136, div. A, title V, §596(c) Additional Matters for Annual Report on Sexual Assaults, Jan. 6, 2006, 119 Stat. 3283 (10 U.S.C. §113 note)."

[14] DoDD 6495.01 and DoDI 6495.02, "Sexual Assault Prevention and Response Program."

[15] DoDD 6495.01 allows a Service member to disclose confidentially the details of a sexual assault to specified individuals and receive medical treatment, counseling, and advocacy services without triggering an investigation. With unrestricted reporting, the individual reports the sexual assault to law enforcement, and the complaint may be used to initiate an investigation. This Directive formally implemented the Restricted and Unrestricted reporting options that had been established by a Directive Type Memorandum from the Under Secretary of Defense (Personnel and Readiness) in June 2005.

a healthcare provider may conduct a sexual assault examination at the complainant's request.

DoD, however, has not established policies or procedures for receiving, processing, or reporting sexual assault complaints from contractor personnel or data concerning such events. The SAPRO Senior Policy Advisor verified that DoD does not have a policy addressing sexual assault advocacy services for complaints from contractor personnel. She said DoD focused specifically on active duty Service members when establishing the Sexual Assault Prevention and Response Program. As a result, sexual assault services are currently available only to active-duty Service members and those persons eligible to receive treatment in military medical treatment facilities.

Contractor employees in Iraq and Afghanistan are only authorized to receive emergency care in military medical treatment facilities.[16] Consequently, there is no requirement to provide them sexual assault services and advocacy programs. However, the sexual assault prevention and response personnel and medical officials we interviewed considered sexual assault medical treatment and follow-on forensic examinations as emergency care, and routinely provided those services to contractor personnel.

The SAPRO Senior Policy Advisor told us there had been some effort, in coordination with the Military Services' Sexual Assault Prevention and Response Program officials, to draft policy language expanding services to include deployed contractor personnel. She said expanding the program to contractors would require revisions to the Federal Acquisition Regulation and Defense Federal Acquisition Regulation, as well as considerations for international and contracting laws.

<u>Sexual Assault Prevention and Response Services Provided to Deployed Contractor Personnel</u>. The Military Services provided sexual assault response services to civilian personnel throughout Iraq and Afghanistan regardless of their employment status. Military Service Sexual Assault Prevention and Response Program managers told us SAPRO had not provided guidance concerning treatment or advocacy services for contractor sexual assault complainants. Program managers told us despite the lack of SAPRO guidance, contractors were provided these services because it was the right thing to do. Military Service Sexual Assault Prevention and Response Program managers considered the program a commander's program, wherein each commander implements the program based on necessary victim care and available resources.

We examined sexual assault prevention and response policies for the Military Services (Army, Navy, Air Force, and Marine Corps) to determine how they implement DoD sexual assault policy guidance and provide treatment to civilians in deployed locations, and how information on advocacy services is collected and reported. Each

---

[16] Defined in DoDI 3020.41, "Contractor Personnel Authorized to Accompany the U.S. Armed Forces", October 3, 2005, paragraph 4.8.2, as resuscitative care, stabilization, hospitalization at Level III Military Treatment Facilities, and assistance with patient movement in emergencies where loss of life, limb, or eyesight could occur.

Service has published policy guidance implementing the DoD Sexual Assault Prevention and Response Program.

As previously noted, DoD did not address the aspects of sexual assault prevention and response services for other categories of complainants such as contractor and civilian personnel. This has created inconsistency in the Military Services' Sexual Assault Prevention and Response Programs regarding who is eligible for services. For example, the Army has included all Army personnel, Army civilians, and family member dependents. The Air Force has included active duty personnel and Air Force civilian employees. The Marine Corps has included all military personnel, regardless of Service branch, and Marine Corps civilians, including Marine Corps contractor personnel. The Navy has included all Service members, all family members, military retirees, and DoD civilian personnel, including DoD contractors.

We interviewed or surveyed 133 Sexual Assault Prevention and Response personnel,[17] including Service program managers, Sexual Assault Review Board members, current and recently deployed SARCs, and VAs at 25 different locations. The consensus among these individuals was that the current DoD sexual assault prevention and response policy is for Service members only, and is not applicable to contractor or civilian employees. However, they were aware that in Iraq and Afghanistan, the practice has been that contractor and civilian employees who report a sexual assault are provided sexual assault response services. Such services include necessary medical treatment, forensic examinations, and the official investigative process. Those interviewed told us they would provide services because they considered it the right thing to do. There was also a consensus that DoD lacks guidance concerning sexual assault complainants who are not active duty Service members.

Data indicate the Army provides most of the sexual assault services in Iraq and Afghanistan. The Army's Sexual Assault Prevention and Response Program is implemented in AR 600-20, "Army Command Policy." Although not addressed in policy, the Army routinely provided sexual assault response services to contractors in Iraq and Afghanistan. We interviewed the Multi National Forces-Iraq (MNF-I) SARC deployed in 2005, and the current MNF-I SARC. They told us the Military Services provided sexual assault response services to contractors. The current MNF-I SARC told us she recently included language in the MNF-I Standard Operating Procedure providing for sexual assault response services for deployed contractors.

We surveyed DSARCs[18] in Iraq regarding sexual assault services then available for U.S. contractor personnel. Of the respondents, 50 percent stated they had provided sexual assault response training to deployed civilians or contractors. A total of 50 percent of respondents said they would offer a contractor complainant the same services offered to a Service member, while 50 percent were either waiting for policy guidance, or could not answer based on not having had a civilian or contractor sexual

---

[17]   Includes Army, Navy, Air Force, and Marine Corps personnel.

[18]   Army, Navy, Air Force, and Marine Corps DSARCs were sent a detailed survey questionnaire.

assault complaint. A total of 90 percent of respondents opined that civilians and contractors would receive victim services.

Additionally, interviews with the Combined Joint Task Force 101 (Afghanistan) DSARC and the Afghanistan DSARC revealed they had expanded their Sexual Assault Prevention and Response Programs to include civilians and contractors through training efforts and by providing DSARC point of contact information to civilians and contractors.

Realizing there was no formal policy on sexual assault response assistance to civilian sexual assault complainants, the Afghanistan DSARC coordinated with local commanding officers to provide services to civilians and contractors. Both Afghanistan DSARCs acknowledged there was no DoD or local command guidance for providing victim services or sexual assault prevention and response training to civilians or contractors. However, they initiated an effort to include contractors in the training program and approximately 60 percent of the Defense contractor companies volunteered to participate.

We also surveyed other DSARCs deployed throughout Afghanistan and asked how they would handle a contractor sexual assault complainant. All respondents indicated civilian and contractor sexual assault complainants would receive victim services and a victim advocate would be assigned to help the complainant.

Contractor Sexual Assault Data Collection and Reporting. SAPRO does not collect information on contractor sexual assault complaints. Therefore, local SARCs had no administrative process to report such services to higher headquarters. SAPRO only tracks sexual assault data where the complainant or accused is an active duty Service member. Although the Military Services provided sexual assault response services to deployed contractor personnel, SAPRO does not routinely receive sexual assault program information on contractor sexual assault complainants from Military Service Sexual Assault Prevention and Response Program officials.

We requested sexual assault program data on 25 contractor sexual assault complaints the MCIOs reported to us.[19] Neither SAPRO nor Military Service Sexual Assault Prevention and Response Program officials were able to give us any program office information regarding the complaints, such as medical treatment or advocacy services provided.

The most reliable information on contractor sexual assault complaints we obtained was from MCIO criminal investigative reports. We found, through information obtained from our interviews and reviews of MCIO case files, instances where military medical treatment facilities provided sexual assault services for contractors, such as medical treatment, sexual assault forensic examinations and advocacy services. However, we were unable to validate advocacy services such as counseling or follow-on medical or mental health treatment. Records are not routinely maintained on contractors

---

[19] Discussed later in the report on page 13.

and there was no mechanism to store, retain, retrieve, or report the sexual assault program information to higher headquarters.

3. Discussion

DoD Directive 6495.01, paragraph 4.1 states, "it is DoD policy to eliminate sexual assault within DoD by providing a culture of prevention, education and training, response capability, victim support, reporting procedures, and accountability that enhances the safety and well-being of all its members."

We found, however, that DoD policy limited sexual assault response to Service members and those eligible for treatment in military medical treatment facilities. Military Service officials consider the SAPR program a commander's program applicable to active duty Service members only. The DoD Sexual Assault Prevention and Response Program and supplemental Military Service policies are military centric, i.e., the protocols, and reporting and treatment options, are uniquely suited to active duty Service members, including activated National Guard and Reserve personnel. SAPRO and Military Services sexual assault program officials are attempting to address the lack of sexual assault prevention and response policy for others comprising the total DoD force.

We concluded from interviews with deployed commanders and Sexual Assault Prevention and Response Program personnel, as well as information in criminal investigative files, that despite current policy limitations, local commanders provided services and care to contractor sexual assault complainants, regardless of their status, though they had no regulatory requirement or authority to do so. Additionally, we found commanders in Iraq and Afghanistan developed local sexual assault response practices, often in reaction to specific incidents, and provided some sexual assault services to contractors, consistent with available resources.

We also concluded that, from mid-2005 to present, SARCs in Iraq and Afghanistan provided care and support to deployed contractors who reported sexual assaults. We found that when a deployed contractor employee reported a sexual assault to military officials, medical care was provided; SARC or Employee Assistance Program assistance was offered to help facilitate victim advocacy services, and a criminal investigation was initiated. While Military Service SARCs provide sexual assault response program services to sexual assault complainants regardless of employment status, they do so without DoD regulatory authority.

B. Are military medical officials required to report sexual assault complaints to law enforcement?

We concluded no DoD or Military Service policy requires medical officials or HCPs to report sexual assault complaints to law enforcement authorities. DoD policy only requires medical officials to notify Sexual Assault Prevention and Response program personnel.

1.   Standards

The applicable standards are from 10 U.S.C. §113 note (2008), "Department of Defense Policy and Procedures on Prevention and Response to Sexual Assaults Involving Members of Armed Forces;" DoD Directive (DoDD) 6495.01, "Sexual Assault Prevention and Response Program," October 6, 2005; DoD Instruction (DoDI) 6495.02, "Sexual Assault Prevention and Response Program," June 23, 2006; Army Regulation (AR) 600-208, "Army Command Policy," March 20, 2008; "Department of the Air Force Instruction 36-6001; Sexual Assault Prevention and Response (SAPR) Program," September 29, 2008; Operational Navy Instruction (OPNAVINST) 1752.1B,"The Sexual Assault Victim Intervention (SAVI) Program," December 29, 2006; Marine Corps Order (MCO) 1752.5, "Sexual Assault Prevention and Response Program," February 05, 2008; and DoD Pamphlet, "Healthcare Provider's Role in Responding to Sexual Assault." These standards are detailed in Appendix B.

2.   Facts

Requirement to Notify Law Enforcement. DoD Pamphlet, "Healthcare Provider's Role in Responding to Sexual Assault," documents the HCP's role as notifying the SARC which allowed:

> the SARC to explain to patients their two reporting options, as well as any available treatment and counseling services. The provider's reporting requirement is met once the SARC has been contacted. Further reporting to law enforcement will be handled by the SARC should the patient choose to make an Unrestricted Report.[20]

To comply with DoD policy, the individual Military Services implemented program policy. Services policies mirrored the DoD policy, including the two reporting options for active duty Service member complainants, and the requirement for the SARC or VA to report the sexual assault complaint to law enforcement for investigation.

Interviews disclosed that military medical treatment facility personnel followed standard protocols in emergency rooms when a sexual assault complainant came into a treatment facility. The admission clerk immediately notified the on-call VA, SARC, or the Sexual Assault Care Coordinator.[21] If the complainant was an active Service member, the SARC or VA advised the complainant about their reporting options. Law enforcement was only notified if the Service member chose to make an unrestricted report. If the complainant was a civilian or contractor, and a SARC was notified, the SARC contacted law enforcement.

We also interviewed a number of deployed personnel, including SARCs, VAs, and HCPs, including obstetricians and gynecologists, as well as Sexual Assault

---

[20] The DoD Pamphlet mentions only "patients" and does not make distinctions between active duty military personnel with restricted and unrestricted reporting options and other patients who have only an unrestricted reporting requirement.

[21] Sexual Assault Care Coordinators are available only at U.S. Army installations.

Prevention and Response Program personnel. It was clear from our interviews that first responders knew sexual assaults involving civilian or contractor personnel required law enforcement notification. Regardless of a complainant's employment status, however, they provided medical care at military medical treatment facilities.

We reviewed sexual assault criminal investigations involving civilians and contractors that occurred in Operations Enduring and Iraqi Freedom areas of operation. Although we could not locate primary Sexual Assault Prevention and Response Program records of services, the criminal investigative files indicated the complainant was provided sexual assault response program and/or medical services. In the criminal investigations we reviewed, medical officials did not notify law enforcement, and as we noted, they were specifically told that such reporting was not their responsibility.

Reporting and Law Enforcement Investigation. Sexual assaults involving contractors in Iraq and Afghanistan were investigated when referred to law enforcement agencies. We reviewed sexual assault investigations involving contractors and civilians that were reported to military law enforcement authorities. We believed this review would assist us in assessing areas such as the medical official's response, Sexual Assault Forensic Evidence (SAFE) kit[22] collection and chain of custody, and the collaboration that occurred between the various military authorities involved.

We obtained the 25 sexual assault criminal investigation files involving civilians and contractors participating in Operations Enduring and Iraqi Freedom Areas of Operations reported in Calendar Years 2005 through 2007. The United States Army Criminal Investigation Command (USACIDC) had 22 investigations. The Naval Criminal Investigative Service (NCIS), together with the Marine Corps Criminal Investigation Division (MCCID), identified three additional investigations. The Air Force Office of Special Investigations (AFOSI) did not have investigations meeting our criteria.

We reviewed the investigations to determine: how the respective MCIOs received complaints; whether Sexual Assault Prevention and Response Program services were provided; whether Victim Witness Assistance Program protocols were followed (i.e., whether complainants were given DoD Forms 2701, "Initial Information for Victims and Witnesses of a Crime"), and to assess compliance with evidence collection, processing, and chain of custody guidance.[23]

The sexual assault complaints included 11 rapes, 13 indecent assaults, and 1 sodomy. Of the 25 allegations, 15 (60 percent) were substantiated, 4 (16 percent) were unsubstantiated, and 6 (24 percent) were undetermined due to insufficient evidence. (See Appendix C for detailed case information).

---

[22] The SAFE kit contains items used by medical personnel for gathering and preserving physical evidence following a sexual assault.

[23] We reviewed the investigations to evaluate DoD sexual assault response policies and procedures for contractors. Our review did not did not evaluate the thoroughness of the investigations.

Despite the lack of program guidance for contractors and civilians, the investigative case files indicated that when medical treatment was required or requested, it was provided. Additionally, in several instances, the case files indicated the contractors and civilians were given SARC and/or VA assistance. Chain of custody was established for evidence when collected, and evidence was processed in accordance with regulatory guidelines.

3. Discussion

DoD Pamphlet, "Healthcare Provider's Role in Responding to Sexual Assault," February 2006, gives very specific guidance that HCPs will not notify law enforcement. This guidance directs HCPs to notify the installation SARC and provides that the health care provider's reporting requirement is met once the SARC has been notified.

C. Do military medical officials comply with standards regarding forensic examinations and medical records maintenance?

As a result of interviews and reviews of 25 investigations, we concluded that medical officials complied with standards regarding the collection, preservation, and chain of custody, for SAFE kits collected as evidence.

We also concluded that the Military Services complied with the DoD policy governing evidence generally, as well as for collecting SAFE kits.

1. Standards

The applicable standards are from 10 U.S.C. §113 note (2008), "Department of Defense Policy and Procedures on Prevention and Response to Sexual Assaults Involving Members of Armed Forces;" DoD Directive (DoDD) 6495.01, "Sexual Assault Prevention and Response Program," October 6, 2005; DoD Instruction (DoDI) 6495.02, "Sexual Assault Prevention and Response Program," June 23, 2006; Army Regulation (AR) 600-208, "Army Command Policy," March 20, 2008; "Department of the Air Force Instruction 36-6001; Sexual Assault Prevention and Response (SAPR) Program," September 29, 2008; Operational Navy Instruction (OPNAVINST) 1752.1B,"The Sexual Assault Victim Intervention (SAVI) Program," December 29, 2006; Marine Corps Order (MCO) 1752.5, "Sexual Assault Prevention and Response Program," February 05, 2008; and Department of Justice, Office of Violence against Women, "National Protocol for Sexual Assault Medical Forensic Examinations," September 2004; Army Regulation 195–5, "Criminal Investigation, Evidence Procedures," June 25, 2007; Air Force OSI Manual 71-122, "Criminal Investigations," August 13, 2007; and Navy Criminal Investigative Service Manual 3, "Criminal Investigations," December 2006. These standards are discussed below and detailed in Appendix B.

2. Facts

We interviewed several current and former individuals involved in the Sexual Assault Prevention and Response Program, ranging from SARCs (installation (CONUS) and deployed), VAs (installation and unit), Military Service Sexual Assault Prevention and Response Program personnel, and medical officials. A consensus from the interviews was that normal operating procedures for a civilian or contractor sexual assault complainant would follow unrestricted reporting guidelines. An unrestricted report would include law enforcement notification. The interviewees indicated that, to the best of their knowledge, if a civilian or contractor complainant consented and a SAFE kit was collected, it would be turned over to law enforcement. While none of the individuals we interviewed had dealt specifically with a sexual assault incident involving a civilian or contractor, each stated an understanding that law enforcement would be notified about a sexual assault complaint from a contractor or civilian.

From interviews with medical officials who were previously deployed, we determined the collection and custody process for SAFE kits was not clearly established for civilian or contractor sexual assault victims in 2005, when the Sexual Assault Prevention and Response Program policy was first established. According to one hospital commander, when he was deployed to Iraq, the procedure included a HCP performing the sexual assault examination, collecting any evidence, and turning the kit over to the Patient Administration Division for transfer to law enforcement. He said the informal protocol identified the Patient Administration Division as the responsible entity for the kit's disposition.

In determining accountability and responsibility for SAFE kits in civilian/contractor sexual assault reports, we reviewed sexual assault investigations involving civilian or contractor complainants. In those investigations, nine kits were collected. An examination of those nine cases revealed the collection, security, preservation, and chain of custody conformed to regulatory requirements. We did not identify any instance where evidence should have been collected, but was not.

3. Discussion

In accordance with DoD policy, the Military Services implemented regulatory requirements for collecting Sexual Assault Forensic Examination kits in cases of restricted and unrestricted reporting. Per DoD requirements, the kit was collected, turned over to law enforcement officers, and stored (1 year for restricted reports). The Navy, Air Force, and Marine Corps required their respective MCIOs to receive and store the kits. The Army required the Provost Marshal Office to do so.

Based on interviews and information obtained from criminal investigative files, we determined that HCPs complied with DoD and Military Service policies for collecting SAFE kits and transferring evidence to law enforcement. First responders knew the requirement to notify law enforcement in sexual assault incidents involving contractors and civilians. They also knew the importance of evidence collection and chain of custody. We did not find any contractor or civilian sexual assault complaint that was reported to law enforcement where evidence collection procedures, if appropriate, were not followed.

D. What are the dispositions of complainants and accused personnel during the investigative process when sexual assault complaints involve contractor personnel?

We concluded that available records did not allow us to determine the disposition of the complainant or the accused during the investigative process.

1.   Standards

None

2.   Facts

DoD MCIO Sexual Assault Case File Data. As previously noted, we obtained a total of 25 sexual assault military criminal investigation files involving civilians and contractors in Iraqi and Afghanistan that were reported in Calendar Years 2005 through 2007. The sexual assault complaints included 11 rapes, 13 indecent assaults, and 1 sodomy. Of the 25 allegations, 15 were substantiated, 4 were unsubstantiated, and 6 were undetermined due to insufficient evidence. Information in the case files provided a disposition on the accused (e.g., terminated, reassigned or received non-judicial punishment) once the allegation was adjudicated. The case files did not contain information that allowed us to determine the disposition of the accused or the complainant during the investigative process.

DoD Contractor Company Sexual Assault Case File Data. Additionally, we identified 10 companies with current DoD contracts.[24] These companies provided a wide range of services including contracts to rebuild and restore the Iraqi electrical grids; product support and training in the areas of intelligence and police training; construction management force protection, public works; and facility maintenance. The companies reported approximately 70 to 2500 employees deployed to Iraq and Afghanistan supporting DoD operations.

We requested the companies provide us information on any sexual assault[25] that occurred in Iraq and Afghanistan involving their employees as either the victim or the accused for Calendar Years 2005 through 2007. Specifically, we requested they provide the following information:

---

[24]   The 10 contractors were selected based on the following criteria: U.S. based companies; contracting actions awarded in FY 2006 and FY 2007; and combined FY 2006 and FY 2007 contracting actions equal to or exceeded $250 million. The contractors reviewed were Kellogg, Brown, and Root Services, Inc. (KBR); AECOM; Tetra Tech, Inc.; Parsons Corporation; Innovative Technical Solutions; Fluor Corporation; Readiness Management Support, LC; Environmental Chemical Corporation; L-3 Communications; and ITT Corporation.

[25]   We provided a comprehensive list of definitions for sexual crimes and sexual misconduct as prescribed in the Uniform Code of Military Justice, Article 120, "Rape, sexual assault, and other sexual misconduct," (2008 Edition), 10 U.S.C. 920."

• Date and location of sexual assault complaint;
• Entity that received the complaint and date received;
• Nature of the sexual assault complaint;
• Description of sexual assault services provided complainant and who provided the services (e.g., military or civilian employee assistance counselor);
• Type of investigation conducted (e.g., criminal or administrative) and by whom;
• Actions taken to physically separate accused and complainant during the investigation;
• Investigation results (e.g., allegation substantiated or not substantiated); and
• Judicial or Administrative action taken.

Nine of the 10 companies reported they had no sexual assault complaints for the time period we requested. One company, KBR, provided us with information on 5 rape complaints.[26] Four of the 5 complaints resulted in a criminal investigation. Three complaints had been reported to and investigated by military law enforcement; 1 complaint was reported to and investigated by the Department of State, Bureau of Diplomatic Security, and 1 complaint was investigated by KBR per their Code of Business Conduct procedures. (See Appendix D for case information).

3. Discussion

Information from the criminal investigative case files we reviewed, and the sexual assault data we received from the contractor, provided a final disposition on the accused (e.g., terminated, returned to home country, received non-judicial punishment) once the allegation was adjudicated. However, we were not able to determine the disposition of the complainant or the accused while the investigation was on-going.

V. CONCLUSIONS

The DoD and Military Service policies and procedures for sexual assault prevention, response, and reporting focus exclusively on Service members who complain about being sexually assaulted. DoD and some Military Service official policies do not address civilian or contractor personnel. Additionally, DoD does not have policies or procedures specific to combat areas. However, the Military Services have procedures that local commanders have expanded in practice to include deployed contractor sexual assault complainants. We found anecdotal and substantive evidence that contractors who reported being sexually assaulted received medical, investigative, and victim advocacy services.

---

[26] KBR told us they used the following definition of rape rather than sexual assault, "act of forced, non-consensual penetration of any bodily orifice (vaginal, anal, or oral) penetration by a body part or inanimate object."

VI. RECOMMENDATIONS

We recommend the Under Secretary of Defense (Personnel and Readiness), establish, and the Military Services implement, policy that will provide an immediate, response, by trained personnel, for all sexual assaults involving U.S. personnel reported to DoD facilities.

We also recommend the Under Secretary of Defense (Personnel and Readiness), Sexual Assault Prevention and Response Program Office, in coordination with the Military Services, develop a data system that records data on sexual assault cases involving civilian and contractor personnel. This data, at minimum, should include the complainant's identity, when and where the assault occurred, when the complaint was filed, the support services requested or provided, when the complaint was referred for criminal investigation, and the final disposition on the complaint.

VII. MANAGEMENT COMMENTS

We received management comments from the office of the Under Secretary of Defense (Personnel and Readiness) on August 27, 2009, concurring with all our recommendations. The full text management comments are included in Appendix F.

Appendix A. DoD Response to Jamie Leigh Jones Sexual Assault Complaint

As noted earlier in this report there was no DoD or Military Services policy that addressed the receiving, processing and reporting of sexual assaults involving contractor personnel at the time of Ms Jones' sexual assault complaint in July 2005. Despite the lack of policy, we concluded that DoD personnel adequately responded to Ms Jones' complaint.

Standards:

Department of Justice, Office of Violence against Women, "National Protocol for Sexual Assault Medical Forensic Examinations," September 2004.

Chapter 6, "Evidence Integrity," Reference (u) provides specific guidance on documenting the handling, transfer and storage of evidence:

> Examiners must maintain control of evidence during the exam, while evidence is being dried, and until it is in the kit container and sealed (and then follow jurisdictional procedures for storing evidence securely or handing it over to a duly authorized agent for transfer to a storage site). Documentation should continue with each transfer of the evidence to law enforcement, the crime laboratory, and others involved in the investigative process. Patients, advocates, family members, and other support persons should not handle the evidence. Documentation of the chain-of-custody information is vital to ensuring that there has been no loss or alteration of evidence prior to trial.

Medical Command Regulation 40-36, "Medical Facility Management," December 23, 2004.

Paragraph 11, Photographers and Equipment, states photographers should be familiar with equipment operation and be educated on forensic photography in sexual assault cases.

Facts:

Based on interviews and data review, we determined that during July 2005, Ms. Jones, a KBR employee deployed to Iraq, and within days of her arrival alleged she was sexually assaulted by fellow KBR employees. Ms. Jones reported the incident to her supervisor who then reported the incident to KBR's Security Office. She was transported to the 86th Combat Support Hospital, Baghdad, Iraq. She was accompanied by her supervisor and a physician assistant from the KBR clinic. Ms. Jones was initially triaged by an emergency room nurse, and later placed in a private room for a sexual assault examination.

The on-call gynecologist, an active duty Army doctor, performed a sexual assault examination on Ms. Jones. The doctor used a standard issued SAFE kit and accompanying forms[27] contained inside the kit to conduct the exam.

During the examination, the doctor noted some bruising and a scratch on Ms. Jones. The doctor documented those injuries on the appropriate sexual assault examination form, and the emergency room medic took approximately 3-5 digital photographs of those injuries using her personal camera.

We asked the doctor and the medic about the Medical Command regulatory requirement that sexual assault photographs be taken by a photographer educated in forensic photography. They both told us they were not aware of any individual assigned to the hospital that was trained in forensic photography. The medic told us she recalled e-mailing the photographs directly to Ms. Jones. She thought she may have also given copies or perhaps e-mailed the photographs to the doctor. We attempted to obtain copies of the photographs, but both the medic and the doctor were unable to locate the photographs.

According to the doctor, the emergency room nurse, and medic, Ms. Jones said she was sexually assaulted by 4-5 firemen, and she did not recall the specific details of the assault until the following morning. The doctor said Ms. Jones indicated the possibility of one of her assailants putting a "Roofie" (more commonly known as rohypnol, the "date rape" drug) in her alcoholic drink. Based on this information, the doctor took urine and blood samples and forwarded them for laboratory examination.

The doctor told us she followed the SAFE kit protocol in collecting the required specimens, and reflected her findings on the protocol checklist and on the hospital's emergency care and treatment form. After completing the examination, she said she placed all specimens collected and accompanying forms back into the SAFE kit, sealed it, and provided the kit to one of the KBR security personnel who had responded to the hospital. Specifically, regarding the SAFE kit and items, she said:

> "I put them back into the box, resealed it, and as usually in the case of the Iraqi security -- I believe they went to the KBR security that was with her [Ms. Jones] as the chain of evidence. I think that most civilian contractors, the kit was handed off to their security, to the best of my recollection."

When asked why she gave the kit to the KBR security personnel she stated:

> "... because they kind of came in and took charge of the people. They kind of came in as security personnel and kinda were their own world. So, I think it was just assumed that they were going to be the security."

When asked if it was standard practice with all contractor personnel to give evidence to contractor security, the doctor told us this was her assumption. She said

---

[27] As noted earlier in the report, the kit contains items used by medical personnel for gathering and preserving physical evidence following a sexual assault.

during her deployment she was not aware of any policies or guidance, written or verbal, regarding procedures for contractor sexual assault complainants.

Discussion:

As reflected earlier in this report, we determined the collection and custody process for SAFE kits was not clearly established for contractor sexual assault victims when Ms. Jones reported her sexual assault in July 2005, and DoD sexual assault policy did not address medical treatment for government contractors. Despite the lack of policy, our review of this case and the other 25 investigations indicated medical health care professionals provided adequate medical care to everyone who reported a sexual assault, including Ms. Jones. The attending doctor told us:

> "There was no guidance given, no. I was under the assumption we treat everyone the same. I don't think we specifically talked about it. I don't think it was ever brought up. But I think just being where we were, we took care of a lot of civilians, a lot of Iraqis, a lot of U.S. military. Actually, U.S. military is probably 50 percent of what we took care of. Nowhere along the way did we ever skimp on care, regardless of who they were, or where they came from."

When Ms. Jones presented to the emergency room complaining of being sexually assaulted, the emergency room nurse triaged her, documented her vital signs on an emergency room intake form, and moved her to a private room. While waiting for her sexual assault examination to be conducted, Ms. Jones was never left alone; either the emergency room nurse or medic remained with her. The doctor responded and consulted with Ms. Jones and obtained her written consent to perform a sexual assault examination.

We reviewed current policy and interviewed medical officials who responded to Ms. Jones' complaint, and determined she received the standard treatment afforded active duty service members. Ms. Jones was separated from other patients and was examined in accordance with the Department of Justice, National Protocol for Sexual Assault Medical Forensic Examinations.

We also coordinated with Department of State officials at the Bureau for Diplomatic Security[28] and examined Ms. Jones' Sexual Assault Forensic Examination kit. Our review disclosed that a proper chain of custody was established and evidence and documents the doctor originally generated were in the kit.[29]

We determined the SAFE kit had been sealed, a chain of custody was established, and KBR security officials released the kit to the appropriate law enforcement agency.

---

[28] Their investigators conducted the criminal investigation of Ms. Jones' sexual assault complaint.

[29] As noted above, the medic took digital photographs with her personal camera that were not included in the SAFE kit.

We contacted the US Attorney's Office (USAO) that conducted the investigation of Ms. Jones' case, and inquired whether they had identified problems or deficiencies with the SAFE kit collection, chain of custody, or preservation. The USAO responded that they had not identified any procedural issues with the collection of evidence that affected their decision on whether to proceed with legal action regarding Ms. Jones' sexual assault complaint.

Although Ms. Jones' SAFE kit was released to her employer, we found that this was due to a lack of established policy governing the proper chain of custody of SAFE kits collected for contractor personnel. We found no specific regulatory guidance for the time period during which Ms. Jones reported her sexual assault (July 2005), addressing contractor related sexual assaults and sexual assault examinations in Iraq. The Under Secretary of Defense (Personnel and Readiness), has directed the Sexual Assault Advisory Council Policy Subcommittee, to establish policy addressing sexual assault assistance to contractors at DoD facilities to include deployed locations. In the interim, deployed commanders have implemented local procedures in theater to care for all sexual assault complainants.

Appendix B. Standards

A. Do DoD policies and procedures address receiving, processing, and reporting sexual assault complaints for contractor personnel in Iraq and Afghanistan?

10 U.S.C. §113 note (2008), "Department of Defense Policy and Procedures on Prevention and Response to Sexual Assaults Involving Members of Armed Forces."

The law required the DoD to develop a comprehensive policy on the prevention of, and response to, sexual assaults involving members of the Armed Forces. The law stipulated the policy must be applicable to, and uniformly implemented by the Military Departments. Elements of the law required the comprehensive policy to address, at minimum, the following:

- sexual assault prevention measures, and education and training on sexual assault prevention and response;

- investigation of complaints by command and law enforcement personnel,

- medical treatment for victims;

- confidential incident reporting;

- victim advocacy and intervention;

- commander oversight on administrative and disciplinary actions responding to substantiated sexual assault incidents;

- disposition of victims of sexual assault, including review by appropriate authority of administrative separation actions involving sexual assault victims;

- disposition of members of the Armed Forces accused of sexual assault;

- liaison and collaboration with civilian agencies on the provision of services to sexual assault victims; and

- uniform data collection on sexual assault incidences and on disciplinary actions taken in substantiated sexual assault cases.

The law further required the Military Departments to prescribe or modify regulations to conform to the DoD comprehensive policy, and ensure that such policies and procedures included the following elements:

- a program to promote awareness of sexual assault incidents involving members of the Armed Forces;

- a program to provide victim advocacy and intervention for Armed Forces members who are sexual assault victims; the program shall make available, at home stations and in deployed locations, trained advocates who are readily available to intervene on behalf of such victims;

- procedures for members of the Armed Force to follow in the case of an incident of sexual assault involving a member of such Armed Force, including—

  - specification of the person or persons to whom the complaint should be reported;

  - specification of any other person whom the complainant should contact;

  - procedures for the preservation of evidence;

  - procedures for confidential reporting and for contacting victim advocates;

  - procedures for disciplinary action in cases of sexual assault by members of the Armed Force concerned;

  - other sanctions authorized to be imposed in substantiated cases of sexual assault; whether forcible or nonforcible, by members of the Armed Force concerned; and

  - training on the policies and procedures for all members of the Armed Force concerned, including specific training for members of the Armed Force concerned who process sexual assault complaints against members of such Armed Force.

DoD Directive (DoDD) 6495.01, "Sexual Assault Prevention and Response Program," October 6, 2005.

This Directive applies to all DoD Components, the Military Departments and Combatant Commands, and established the DoD comprehensive policy on prevention and response to sexual assaults.

Paragraph 4, "Policy," Subparagraph 4.1., states that "it is DoD policy to eliminate sexual assault within the Department of Defense by providing a culture of prevention, education and training, response capability, victim support, reporting procedures, and accountability that enhances the safety and well-being of all its members."

DoD Instruction (DoDI) 6495.02, "Sexual Assault Prevention and Response Program," June 23, 2006.

The Instruction consolidated the DoD sexual assault program policy under the Under Secretary of Defense (Personnel and Readiness), Sexual Assault Prevention and Response Program Office (SAPRO), for implementation.

Paragraph 2, "Applicability and Scope," Subparagraphs 2.1., 2.2., and 2.4., apply this Instruction to the DoD components, National Guard and Reserve members who are sexually assaulted when performing active service and inactive duty training, and any person who is a sexual assault victim and eligible to receive treatment in Military Medical Treatment Facilities.

The Directive and Instruction constitutes the DoD policy on sexual assault prevention and response.

Army Regulation 600-20, "Army Command Policy," March 20, 2008.

This Regulation implements the DoD Sexual Assault and Prevention and Response program for the Department of the Army. Chapter 8, "Sexual Assault Prevention and Response Program," provides the policy guidance for the Army's Sexual Assault Prevention and Response program. Subparagraph 8-1 describes the program purposes and goals. It states "the goals of the Sexual Assault Prevention and Response Program are to create a climate that minimizes sexual assault incidents, which impact Army personnel, Army civilians, and family members, and, if an incident should occur, ensures that victims and subjects [accused] are treated according to Army policy."

Air Force Policy Directive 36-60, "Sexual Assault Prevention and Response Program," March 28, 2008.

This Directive implements the DoD Sexual Assault and Prevention and Response program for the Department of the Air Force, and applies to all levels of command and all Air Force organizations, including Active Duty, civilians, Air Force Academy, Air National Guard, and Air Force Reserve components while in Federal service. The directive provides policy and assigns responsibility for preventing and responding to sexual assault. It also establishes command relationships, authorities, and responsibilities. Chapter 1 "Policy," Subparagraph 1.1., states it is Air Force policy to "eliminate sexual assault within the Department of the Air Force by fostering a culture of prevention, providing education and training, response capability, victim support, reporting procedures, and accountability that enhances the safety and well-being of all its members."

"Department of the Air Force Instruction 36-6001; Sexual Assault Prevention and Response (SAPR) Program," September 29, 2008.

This instruction implements Air Force Policy Directive (AFPD) 36-60, 28 March 2008, *Sexual Assault Prevention and Response (SAPR) Program*, and Department of Defense Instruction (DoDI) 6495.02, 23 June 2006, *Sexual Assault Prevention and Response (SAPR) Program Procedures*. It assigns responsibility for the prevention of and response to sexual assault and establishes command relationships, authorities and responsibilities in support of the policy. This instruction applies to all levels of command and all Air Force organizations including the Active Duty, Air Force government civilian employees, Air Force Academy, and Air National Guard and Air Force Reserve components while in Federal service. It addresses the requirements of the Ronald W. Reagan National Defense Authorization Act for fiscal year 2005, P.L. 108-375, as amended and supplemented, 28

October 2004, Section 577(e). Failure to observe the prohibitions and mandatory provisions of this instruction in paragraphs 2.12.1., regarding the requirement to report sexual assaults, and paragraph 3.1.9., and its sub paragraphs regarding safeguarding covered communications, is a violation of Article 92, *Uniform Code of Military Justice* (UCMJ). Violations may result in administrative disciplinary action without regard to otherwise applicable criminal or civil sanctions for violations of related laws. Violations by civilian employees may result in administrative disciplinary action without regard to otherwise applicable criminal or civil sanctions for violations of related laws. Violations by contactor personnel will be handled according to local laws and the terms of the contract.

Operational Navy Instruction 1752.1B,"The Sexual Assault Victim Intervention (SAVI) Program," December 29, 2006.

This Instruction implements the DoD Sexual Assault and Prevention and Response program for the Department of the Navy. Chapter 6 "Policy," states "the goal of the Navy is to reduce sexual assault by providing a culture of prevention, education, and training response capability, victim support, reporting procedures, and accountability that enhances the safety and well-being of all." Chapter 7 "Applicability," applies the sexual assault program to:

a. Active duty members of the Military Services (Army, Navy, Air Force, Marine Corps, and Coast Guard, when operating as a Service in the Navy,) who are eligible to receive treatment in a Military Treatment Facility and their legal family members;

b. Members of the National Guard and Reserve component of the Military Services and their legal family members when performing active services and inactive duty training;

c. On a space-available basis, retired members of the Military Services and their legal family members;

d. Non-foreign-hire DoD civilian employees in overseas locations, and their legal family members, for services that are not available in the local community; and

e. Victims of sexual assault incidents occurring under Department of the Navy jurisdiction are eligible, regardless of affiliation, for available advocacy services on a humanitarian basis.

Marine Corps Order (MCO) 1752.5, "Sexual Assault Prevention and Response Program," February 05, 2008.

This Order implements the DoD Sexual Assault and Prevention and Response Program for the Marine Corps and defines and assigns specific responsibilities throughout the Marine Corps for sexual assault prevention and response. It applies to all Marines, Marine Reservists (active duty/drilling status), Armed Forces personnel attached to or serving with Marine Corps commands, civilian Marines, and contractors employed by the Marine Corps. Paragraph 1, "Purpose," "establishes Marine Corps policy and guidance to address specific sexual assault victim needs and related issues by defining sexual assault and required reporting procedures; establish procedures to protect the victim's privacy; and establish a mandatory, standardized sexual assault victim assistance program for Service members." Paragraph 7, "Applicability," applies the guidance to the Marine Corps Total Force.

Multi National Forces –Iraq /Multi National Corps-Iraq Human Relations & Equal Opportunity Program Manager and Theater Deployable Sexual Assault Response Coordinator Draft Standard Operating Procedures, "Multi-National Corps-Iraq Sexual Assault Prevention and Response Program."

This draft Standard Operating Procedure implements the Multi-National Corps-Iraq Sexual Assault Prevention and Response Program specifically for the Iraqi area of operations. The guidance states "the program's purpose is to help prevent sexual assault in the Iraq area of operation, explain commander responsibilities, and provide information on available resources to help commanders if a sexual assault occurs."

Further, Paragraph 11b, directs that "any Federal civilian employee or contract employee who is an alleged victim of sexual assault, will be offered a preliminary medical evaluation at the closest Military Treatment Facility." It goes on to say "law enforcement officers will be contacted immediately and law enforcement procedures will be strictly enforced."

B. Are military medical officials required to report sexual assault complaints to law enforcement?

DoD Pamphlet, "Healthcare Provider's Role in Responding to Sexual Assault," February 2006.

The pamphlet directs HCP's to take the following action when managing incidents of sexual assault:

> "Reporting and Care"....
>
> In most situations, the military requires providers to notify law enforcement when patients report being the victim of a crime. However, in cases of sexual assault, providers should NOT notify law enforcement. Instead, you should notify the Sexual Assault Response Coordinator (SARC) for your installation."

C. Do military medical officials comply with standards regarding forensic examinations and medical records maintenance?

DoD Directive 6495.01 "Sexual Assault Prevention and Response Program," October 6, 2005.

The Directive defines the "Sexual Assault Forensic Examination" as:

> The medical examination of a sexual assault victim under circumstances and controlled procedures to ensure the physical examination process, and the

collection, handling, analysis, testing, and safekeeping of any bodily specimens, meet the requirements necessary for use as evidence in criminal proceedings.

DoD Instruction 6495.02, "Sexual Assault Prevention and Response Program Procedures," Jun 23, 2006.

Additionally the Instruction discusses the procedures for the collection of Sexual Assault Forensic Examination kits:

> Sexual assault reporting procedures require that the SARC be notified of all incidents of reported sexual assault. The SARC, in turn, will assign a VA to assist the victim. The SARC or VA shall also inform the victim about the availability of an optional Sexual Assault Forensic Examination. If a victim chooses to undergo a Sexual Assault Forensic Examination, and the HCP determines a Sexual Assault Forensic Examination is indicated by the facts of the case, HCPs at military facilities shall conduct the examination according to the most current version of Reference (u) and other applicable community standards of care.

Department of Justice, Office of Violence against Women, "National Protocol for Sexual Assault Medical Forensic Examinations," September 2004.

Chapter 6, "Evidence Integrity," Reference (u) provides specific guidance on documenting the handling, transfer and storage of evidence:

> Examiners must maintain control of evidence during the exam, while evidence is being dried, and until it is in the kit container and sealed (and then follow jurisdictional procedures for storing evidence securely or handing it over to a duly authorized agent for transfer to a storage site). Documentation should continue with each transfer of the evidence to law enforcement, the crime laboratory, and others involved in the investigative process. Patients, advocates, family members, and other support persons should not handle the evidence. Documentation of the chain-of-custody information is vital to ensuring that there has been no loss or alteration of evidence prior to trial. Educate all those involved in handling, transferring, and storing evidence regarding the specifics of maintaining the chain of custody.

Army Regulation 195–5, "Criminal Investigation, Evidence Procedures," June 25, 2007.

Chapter 2, "Recording and Accountability of Evidence", Paragraph 2–15b, Procedures for restricted or unrestricted reporting states that:

> In sexual assault cases, additional forensic evidence may be collected using the Sexual Assault Evidence Collection Kit, (referred to hereafter as evidence kit) or a suitable substitute. The Military Treatment Facility, SARC, VA, or chaplain will have only temporary possession of the evidence and must immediately notify the installation Provost Marshal office to transfer custody of evidence. The evidence kit, other items such as clothing or bedding sheets, and

any other articles provided by the Military Treatment Facility, SARC, VA, or chaplain will be stored in the installation Provost Marshal's evidence room separate from other evidence and property.

The first law enforcement officer receiving the evidence kit or other items will initiate a Department of the Army Form 4137 (Evidence/Property Custody Document). Law enforcement personnel will have the Military Treatment Facility, SARC, VA, or chaplain sign the Department of the Army Form 4137 releasing the items to law enforcement. Procedures for handling evidence specified in this regulation will be strictly followed.

Air Force OSI Manual 71-122, "Criminal Investigations," August 13, 2007.

Chapter 2.12.2, "Sexual Assault Investigations under Restricted and Unrestricted Reporting," paragraph 2.12.2.5.4 "Collection and Preservation of Evidence Under Restricted Reporting," states that:

When the SARC receives a restricted report of a sexual assault, the victim will be informed of the availability of healthcare, including the option of undergoing a sexual assault forensic examination (SAFE) and the collection of evidence. When authorized by the victim, the SARC or VA will arrange for the SAFE to be conducted by properly qualified medical personnel and evidence will be processed in a manner that preserves forensic viability and affords a valid chain of custody, yet maintains victim confidentiality.

SARCs and host command authorities are responsible for coordinating and resolving any issues with local hospitals that will not conduct a SAFE without the initiation of an official investigation.

AFOSI detachments will receive and store SAFE kits and any bags containing clothes or other evidence collected from the victim under restricted reporting. Detachments should coordinate with their local SARCs to establish procedures for receiving evidence. SAFE kits and all evidence collected should be immediately turned over to AFOSI to avoid chain of custody issues. According to DoDI 6495.02, AFOSI should receive kits directly from HCPs; however, AFOSI will not refuse a SAFE kit received from a SARC (or his or her designee).

Navy Criminal Investigative Service Manual 3, "Criminal Investigations," December 2006.

Chapter 34, "DOD Policy on Restricted Reports of Sexual Assault," paragraph 4.9b states that:

Physical Evidence. With the victim's consent, medical providers can utilize a physical evidence recovery kit to obtain evidence of a sexual assault. Non-identifying information will be placed on the outside of the kit, which will eventually be turned over to NCIS if the victim later elects to make an unrestricted report of the sexual assault. The Sexual Assault Evidence (SAE)

Collection Kit may become an integral aspect of a sexual assault investigation if the victim later opts to make an unrestricted report. Since law enforcement is not involved in restricted reporting, medical personnel involved in the care of a victim may collect items of potential evidentiary value in the SAE Kit. The completed SAE Kit will be sealed by medical personnel and mailed to the NCIS Consolidated Evidence Facility in Norfolk, VA (the long term evidence storage facility) within 48 hours of the evidence collection. Documentation generated during the examination shall be placed in a plastic bag and sealed inside the SAE Kit. The SAE Kit may also include photographic images saved to a compact disc and wet prep materials. A completed chain of custody will accompany the SAE Kit. In addition, the VA/SARC will provide a Restricted Reporting Case Number (RRCN) for the SAE Kit and notify the NCIS Consolidated Evidence Facility, Norfolk, VA via an e-mail message when the SAE Kit has been mailed. If a victim or healthcare provider suspects a drug facilitated sexual assault, a separate Drug Facilitated Sexual Assault (DFSA) Kit will be utilized in addition to the SAE Kit. SAE and DFSA Kits received at the Norfolk Consolidated Evidence Facility will be stored for a period of one year. If after 12 months a victim has not communicated their desire to change their restricted report to unrestricted, the kits stored at the NCIS Consolidated Evidence Facility will be destroyed.

Appendix C. MCIO Case Data

Case Number	Offense	Date of Occurrence	Location	Legal Finding	Case/Offender Disp	SARC	EAP	DD Form 2701	SAFE Kit
1	Sodomy	21-Apr-05	KBR Village, Bagram AB, AFGHAN	Insufficient Evidence	Insufficient Evidence	Not Indicated	Not Indicated	Not Indicated	Yes
2	Indecent Assault	4-May-05	PX Station, Cp Liberty, IZ	Substantiated	Terminated	Not Indicated	Not Indicated	Yes	N/A
3	Indecent Assault	28-May-05	FOB Lima, Karbala, IZ	Insufficient Evidence	Insufficient Evidence	Not Indicated	Not Indicated	Not Indicated	N/A
4	Rape	13-Sep-05	Housing Unit, FOB Endurance, Mosul, IZ	Unsubstantiated	Insufficient Evidence	Not Indicated	Not Indicated	Not Indicated	Yes
5	Rape	21-Oct-05	Apt, Tower B, Kuwait City, KUWAIT	Insufficient Evidence	Insufficient Evidence	Yes	Yes	Not Indicated	Yes
6	Rape	15-Dec-05	Qtrs, Joint Ops Compound, Bagram, AFGHAN	Unsubstantiated	Insufficient Evidence	Yes	Yes	Not Indicated	Yes
7	Rape	24-Nov-05	Trailer, Dodge City South, Cp Victory, Baghdad, IZ	Unsubstantiated	Unsubstantiated	Not Indicated	Not Indicated	Not Indicated	N/A
8	Indecent Assault	16-Nov-05	MWR Bldg, FOB Honor, Baghdad, IZ	Substantiated	Non-judicial Punishment	Not Indicated	Not Indicated	Not Indicated	N/A
9	Indecent Assault	12-Jul-05	Trailer, Cp Liberty IZ	Substantiated	Terminated	Not Indicated	Not Indicated	Not Indicated	N/A
10	Rape	22-Dec-05	Camp Ramadi, IZ	Substantiated	Pending Prosecution	Not Indicated	Not Indicated	Not Indicated	Yes
11	Indecent Assault	20-Mar-05	Al Asad AB, IZ	Substantiated	Terminated	Not Indicated	Not Indicated	Not Indicated	N/A
End of CY05									
12	Indecent Assault	26-Feb-06	Next to Mess Hall, Cp Scania, Nippur, IZ	Insufficient Evidence	Insufficient Evidence	Not Indicated	Not Indicated	Yes	N/A
13	Indecent Assault	12-Jun-06	Dining Facility, Cp Cedar II, Tallil, IZ	Substantiated	Terminated	Yes	Not Indicated	Yes	N/A
14	Rape	26-Mar-06	Office, COB Speicher, Tikrit, IZ	Substantiated	Terminated	Yes	Yes	Yes	Yes
15	Indecent Assault	19-May-06	PX Spa, COB Speicher, Tikrit, IZ	Substantiated	Terminated	Not Indicated	Not Indicated	Yes	No
16	Rape	25-Jan-06	Trailer, Cp Victory, Baghdad, IZ	Insufficient Evidence	Insufficient Evidence	Not Indicated	Yes	Not Indicated	No
17	Indecent Assault	5-Aug-06	MWR Bldg, Cp Arifjan, Kuwait	Substantiated	Non-judicial Punishment	Offered but declined	Offered but declined	Yes	N/A
18	Rape	22-Jun-06	Trailer, Cp Victory, Baghdad, IZ	Insufficient Evidence	Insufficient Evidence	Not Indicated	Yes	Yes	No. Reported 3 months late
19	Indecent Assault	1-Sep-06	Trailer, Cp Victory, Baghdad, IZ	Substantiated	Terminated	Not Indicated	Yes	Yes	N/A
20	Indecent Assault	14-Dec-06	Laundry Bldg, Bagram Airfield, Afghanistan	Substantiated	Terminated	Not Indicated	Not Indicated	Yes	N/A
21	Rape	Not Reported	Al Asad AB, IZ	Insufficient Evidence	Insufficient Evidence	Offered but declined	Offered but declined	Yes	Yes
End of CY06									
22	Rape	23-Feb-07	KBR Life Spt Area, Cp Stryker, Baghdad, IZ	Substantiated	Pending Prosecution	Offered but declined	Yes	Yes	No. Victim declined
23	Indecent Assault	3-Mar-07	Air Terminal, LSA Anaconda, Balad, IZ	Substantiated	Reassigned	Offered but declined	Offered but declined	Yes	N/A
24	Rape	25-Jul-07	Qtrs, Cp Eggers, Afghanistan	Unsubstantiated	Unsubstantiated	Yes	Yes	Not Indicated	No. Allegation Unsub
25	Indecent Assault	1-Sep-07	Room, KBR Compound, LSA Anaconda, Balad, IZ	Substantiated	Terminated	Yes	Yes	Yes	N/A
End of CY 07									

Highlighted cases indicate complaints that involve a contractor complainant and contractor offender.

Appendix D. KBR Case Data

1. Location and Date – USMI Main 7/28/2005 (Information provided in previously produced documentation – Jamie Leigh Jones)

2. Location and Date – B-Sites (Information provided in previously produced documentation – Pending Prosecution)

3. Location and Date – Camp Victory 1/25 or 26/2006

    a. Entity that received the complaint and date received

    Complainant initially reported the alleged incident described in item b below via the KBR DRP in mid-February 2006. The DRP referred the matter to Employee Relations in Houston, who then communicated the report to the legal department, which commenced a KBR Security Investigation per COBC procedures.

    b. Nature of complaint

    Complainant alleged that while waiting to talk to Employee Relations about her separation of employment (which had been communicated to her earlier), complainant sought out the accused at his office and then accompanied him to his room voluntarily where he sexually assaulted her. Thereafter, they ate lunch together in the DFAC. The accused admitted sexual relations on that occasion but stated that it was consensual.

    c. Description of services provided and who provided the services

    None noted in file. Complainant was no longer in theater or an employee when she reported the incident.

    d. Type of investigation conducted and by whom

    KBR Security Investigations per COBC procedures.

    e. Actions taken to physically separate the accused and the victim

    None needed since complainant had demobilized prior to reporting the incident.

    f. Investigation results

    Complainant's allegation could not be substantiated.

g. Judicial or administrative action taken

Complainant filed a claim through the KBR DRP which was settled prior to arbitration.

4. Location and Date – B-Sites 6/21 or 22/2006

   a. Entity that received the complaint and date received

   Complainant reported the alleged incident described in item b below to KBR Security on September 2, 2006.

   b. Nature of complaint

   Complainant first alleged on September 2, 2006, in the course of an investigation of a complaint brought by another employee against the accused, that the accused had made several sexual advances towards her which she refused, including one night when he came to her living container to talk about a death in his family. On September 6, complainant changed her prior statement and said that the accused had raped her on either June 21 or 22, the night he came into her living container to talk about a death in his family.

   c. Description of services provided and who provided the services

   None noted in file.

   d. Type of investigation conducted and by whom

   KBR Security Investigation per COBC procedures. Incident reported to CID which performed its own investigation.

   e. Actions taken to physically separate the accused and the victim

   None needed because accused had been terminated before complainant raised the allegation of rape.

   f. Investigation results

   Complainant's allegation could not be substantiated.

   g. Judicial or administrative action taken

   Complainant filed a claim through the KBR DRP which was settled at mediation.

5. Location and Date – D-5 2/23/2007

    a. Entity that received the complaint and date received

    Complainant reported the alleged incident described in item b below to KBR Security and the KBR Medical Department on February 24, 2007.

    b. Nature of complaint

    Complainant alleged she had consensual sexual relations with the accused on two occasions prior to the alleged assault (on 2/13 and 2/15 or 16) but was seeing someone else and decided to stop having sexual relations with the accused. Complainant entered the accused's living container where they kissed and engaged in oral sex consensually but complainant alleged that the sexual intercourse that followed was not consensual.

    c. Description of services provided and who provided the services

    Complainant was seen but not medically examined by a KBR Medic, who with a KBR Security Technician reported the allegation to the Camp Striker Mayor's Cell. CID and military police personnel arrived immediately and took a report from the KBR Medic and Security Technician. Complainant refused an offer of medical treatment from a military physician. Complainant received counseling services from the KBR EAP.

    d. Type of investigation conducted and by whom

    Internal investigation conducted by KBR Employee Relations. CID conducted its own investigation.

    e. Actions taken to physically separate the accused and the victim

    The accused transferred to a different site.

    f. Investigation results

    CID concluded there was not sufficient evidence to refer case to Department of Justice under Military Extraterritorial Jurisdiction Act ("MEJA").

    g. Judicial or administrative action taken

    No actions filed against KBR.

Appendix E. Report Distribution

Office of the Secretary of Defense

Under Secretary of Defense for Personnel and Readiness

Director, DoD Sexual Assault Prevention and Response Office*

General Counsel, Department of Defense

Military Departments

Inspector General, Department of the Army

Commander, U.S. Army Criminal Investigation Command

Naval Inspector General

Director, Naval Criminal Investigative Service

Inspector General, Department of the Air Force

Commander, Air Force Office of Special Investigations

Congressional Committees and Subcommittees, Chairman and Ranking Minority Members

Senate Committee on Appropriations

Senate Subcommittee on Defense, Committee on Appropriations

Senate Committee on Armed Services

Senate Committee on Governmental Affairs

House Committee on Appropriations

House Subcommittee on Defense, Committee on Appropriations

House Committee on Armed Services

House Committee on Government Reform

House Subcommittee on Government Efficiency, Financial Management, and Intergovernmental Relations, Committee on Government Reform

House Subcommittee on National Security, Veterans Affairs, and International Relations, Committee on Government Reform

*Recipient of draft report

Appendix F. Management Comments

OFFICE OF THE UNDER SECRETARY OF DEFENSE
4000 DEFENSE PENTAGON
WASHINGTON, DC 20301-4000

PERSONNEL AND
READINESS

AUG 27

MEMORANDUM FOR INSPECTOR GENERAL OF THE DEPARTMENT OF DEFENSE

SUBJECT: Comments on "Evaluation of DoD Sexual Assault Response in Operations
Enduring and Iraqi Freedom Areas of Operation" Project No. 2008C003

The Department has the following comments on recommendations made in the report:

Recommendation: We recommend the Under Secretary of Defense (Personnel
and Readiness) establish, and the Military Services implement, policy that will
provide an immediate response by trained personnel for all sexual assault reports
presented at DoD facilities, including those at deployed locations.

Response: **Concur.**

Comment: While the Department does allow for provision of services for all
overseas victims of crime regardless of military, civilian employee or contractor
status under DoD Instruction 1030.02, Paragraph E2.1.5.2, the Department would
benefit from specific guidance as it pertains to sexual assault crimes. I will direct
the Sexual Assault Advisory Council Policy Subcommittee to draft language that
addresses assistance to civilian employees and civilian contractors at DoD
facilities, including those at deployed locations. The background work on this
policy has begun and we were waiting for the results of your evaluation before
proceeding. It is expected that policy addressing civilian employees can be
established in FY2010. However, policy pertaining to civilian contractors must be
coordinated with changes to the Federal Acquisition Regulation and the Defense
Federal Acquisition Regulation, which may require substantially more time.

Recommendation: We also recommend the Under Secretary of Defense
(Personnel and Readiness), in coordination with the Military Services, develop a
data system that records relevant data on sexual assault cases involving civilian
and contractor personnel. This data, at minimum, should include the
complainant's identity, when and where the assault occurred, when the complaint
was filed, the support services requested or provided, when the complaint was
referred for criminal investigation, and the final disposition on the complaint.

Response: **Concur.**

Comment: The Sexual Assault Prevention and Response Office has already included the requested data elements pertaining to civilian employees and contractor personnel into the Defense Sexual Assault Incident Database (DSAID). DSAID is currently in the development process, and is expected to begin its phased implementation during FY2010.

Gail H. McGinn
Deputy Under Secretary of Defense (Plans)
Performing the Duties of the
    Under Secretary of Defense
    (Personnel and Readiness)

Office of the Undersecretary of Defense, (Personnel and Readiness) Comments